Woolridge Surname

Ireland: 1600s to 1900s

From Ireland Church Records of Baptism, Marriage and Death

Comprised of Roman Catholic and Church of Ireland Records

From Counties Carlow, Cork, Kerry and Dublin City

Compiled by **Donovan Hurst**

February 28, 2013

ISBN: 1939958067
ISBN-13: 978-1-939958-06-8

Dedication

This work is dedicated to all of those that came before us and shaped our lives to make us the people that we are today.

Table of Contents

Introduction

This is a compilation of individuals who have the surname of Woolridge that lived in the country of Ireland from the 1600s to the 1900s. I have placed each entry into one of four categories: Families, Individual Births/Baptisms, Individual Burials, and Individual Marriages. If a marriage entry primarily concerns an Individual Woolridge whom is female, then I have placed that entry under the category of Individual Marriages. If a marriage entry primarily concerns an Individual Woolridge whom is male, then I have placed that entry under the category of Families. Images of many of these listings are available at http://churchrecords.irishgenealogy.ie/churchrecords/.

To help guide the reader of this work, the format of this book is as follows:

- Main Family Entry (Husband and Wife) (Father and Mother)

  - Child of Main Family Entry, including Spouse(s) when available

    - Grandchild of Main Family Entry, including Spouse(s) when available

      - Great-Grandchild of Main Family Entry, including Spouse(s) when available

(Bolded Text) following any entry includes any additional information such as Residence(s), Occupation(s), Signature(s), etc. when available.

Hurst

Some of the fonts used in this work symbolizes Celtic writing. The traditional letters, numbers, and punctuation marks and their Celtic counterparts are as follows:

Traditional Letters (Uppercase & Lowercase)

A a B b C c D d E f G g H h I i J j K k L l M m N n O o P p Q q R r S s T t U u V v W w X x Y y Z z

Celtic Letters (Uppercase & Lowercase)

A a B b C c D ð E e F ꜰ G g H h I í J ȷ K k L l M m

N n O o P p Q q R ʀ S s T t U u V ʋ W ѡ X x Y ẏ Z z

Traditional Numbers

1 2 3 4 5 6 7 8 9 10

Celtic Numbers

1 2 3 4 5 6 7 8 9 10

Traditional Punctuation

. , : ‘ “ & - ( )

Celtic Punctuation

. , : ‘ “ & - ( )

Parish Churches

Dublin (Church of Ireland)

St. Catherine Parish, St. Mark Parish, St. Nicholas Within Parish, St. Paul Parish, and St. Peter Parish.

Dublin (Roman Catholic or RC)

SS. Michael & John Parish, St. Michan Parish, and St. Nicholas Parish.

Families

- Henry Woolridge & Alice Unknown

  o Mary Woolridge – bapt. 15 Dec 1749 (Baptism, **St. Michan Parish (RC)**)

- Hugh Woolridge & Margaret Cameron – 20 May 1782 (Marriage, **St. Catherine Parish**)

- Hugh Woolridge & Margaret Gamble – 2 Jun 1782 (Marriage, **St. Catherine Parish**)

- Richard Woolridge & Anne Collins

  o George Woolridge – b. 19 Feb 1858, bapt. 19 Mar 1858 (Baptism, **St. Nicholas Parish (RC)**)

Richard Woolridge (father):

Residence - 9 Little Ship Street - March 19, 1858

- Richard Woolridge & Anne Woolridge

  o John Woolridge – bapt. 12 Mar 1795 (Baptism, **St. Mark Parish**)

Richard Woolridge (father):

Residence - City Quay - March 12, 1795

Hurst

- Richard Woolridge & Unknown

  o Anne Woolridge &William Free (2nd Marriage) – 1 Apr 1861 (Marriage, **St. Catherine Parish**)

Signatures:

Anne Woolridge (daughter):

    Residence - Green Villa Avenue - April 1, 1861

    Relationship Status at Marriage - minor

William Free, son of John Free (son-in-law):

    Residence - Love Lane - April 1, 1861

    Occupation - Gardener - April 1, 1861

    Relationship Status at Marriage - widow

John Free (father):

    Occupation - Farmer

Richard Woolridge (father):

    Occupation - Farmer

Woolridge Surname Ireland: 1600s to 1900s

Wedding Witnesses:

James Lyons & John Fletcher Free

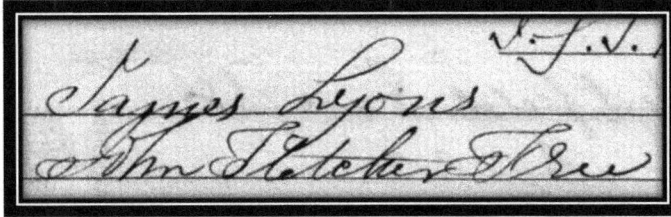

Signatures:

- Thomas Woolridge & Frances Unknown

    o   Frances Woolridge – bapt. 3 Nov 1789 (Baptism, **St. Nicholas Within Parish**)

    o   Martha Woolridge – bapt. 3 Jan 1791 (Baptism, **St. Nicholas Within Parish**)

    o   Thomas Woolridge – b. 2 Jan 1796, bapt. 6 Jan 1796 (Baptism, **St. Nicholas Within Parish**)

Hurst

- William Woolridge & Unknown

    - George Woolridge & Bridget Broderick – 19 Oct 1857 (Marriage, **St. Peter Parish**)

Signatures:

George Woolridge (son):

   Residence - Portobello Barracks - October 19, 1857

   Occupation - Gunner, Royal Artillery - October 19, 1857

Bridget Broderick, daughter of Martin Broderick (daughter-in-law):

   Residence - 7 Lower Fitzwilliam Street - October 19, 1857

Martin Broderick (father):

   Occupation - Laborer

William Woolridge (father):

   Occupation - Steward

Woolridge Surname Ireland: 1600s to 1900s

Wedding Witnesses:

Richard Studdert & Matilda Bodle

Signatures:

Individual Baptisms/Births

None Were Listed

Individual Burials

- Charles Woolridge – b. 1818, bur. 1 Apr 1846 (Burial, **Paul Parish**)

Charles Woolridge (deceased):

  Residence - Royal Barracks - before April 1, 1846

  Occupation - Private, 70th Regiment - before April 1, 1846

  Age at Death - 28 years

- Robert Woolridge – bur. 19 Jan 1768 (Burial, **St. Peter Parish**)

Individual Marriages

- Mary Woolridge & Henry Forbes

  o Mary Forbes – bapt. 16 Feb 1809 (Baptism, **SS. Michael & John Parish** (RC))

- Mary Woolridge & James Curren

  o Catherine Curren – bapt. 3 Jan 1819 (Baptism, **SS. Michael & John Parish** (RC))

- Mary Woolridge & John Smith

  o Mary Smith – b. 6 Aug 1886, bapt. 16 Aug 1886 (Baptism, **St. Michan Parish** (RC))

John Smith (father):

Residence - 127 Upper Dorset Street - August 16, 1886

Woolridge Surname Ireland: 1600s to 1900s

Name Variations

Includes Latin and Abbreviated forms of names found in the original documents.

Abigail = Abigale, Abigall

Anne = Ann, Anna, Annae

Bartholomew = Barth, Bartholmeus, Bartholomeo

Bridget = Birgis, Brigid, Brigida, Bridgit

Catherine = Catharine, Catharina, Catharinae, Catherina, Cath, Catha, Cathae, Cathe, Cathn, Kate

Charles = Carolus, Charls, Chas

Christopher = Christoph

Daniel = Danielem, Danielis

Edmund = Edmond

Edward = Ed, Edwd

Eleanor = Eleo, Eleonora, Elinor, Ellenor

Elizabeth = Betty, Elisa, Elisabeth, Eliz, Eliza, Elizab, Elizh, Elizth

Ellen = Elena, Ellena

Emily = Emilia

Esther = Essie, Ester

Francis = Fransicum

George = Geo, Georg, Georgius

Grace = Gratiae

Gulielmo = Guil, Guillelmi, Gulielmum, Guillelmus, Gulmi

Helen = Helena

Woolridge Surname Ireland: 1600s to 1900s

Honor = Hanora, Honora

James = Jacobi, Jacobus, Jas

Jane = Joanna

Jeanne = Jeannae, Joannae

Joan = Johanna, Joney

John = Jno, Joannem, Joannes, Johannis

Joseph = Jos

Juliana = Julian

Leticia = Letitia, Lettice, Letticia

Lewis = Louis

Luke = Lucas

Margaret = Margarita, Margaritae, Margeret, Marget, Margt

Martha = Marthae

Mary = Maria, My

Mary Anne = Marianna, Marianne, Maryanne

Michael = Michaelis, Michl

Patrick = Pat, Patt, Patk, Patricii, Patricius

Peter = Petri

Richard = Ricardi, Ricardus, Rich, Richd

Robert = Roberti

Rose = Rosa, Rosae

Thomas = Thom, Thomae, Thoms, Thos, Ths

Timothy = Timotheus, Timy

William = Wil, Will, Willm, Wm

Notes

Notes

Notes

Notes

Notes

Notes

Index

Woolridge Surname Ireland: 1600s to 1900s

About The Author

Donovan Hurst graduated from San Diego State University with a Bachelor of Arts in the major field of studies of History and a minor in the field of studies of Anthropology. He is a current member of The General Society of Mayflower Descendants and has been conducting genealogical research for over 10 years tracing back his ancestors to their ancestral homelands in Denmark, England, France, Germany, Ireland, Norway, and Scotland.